The Magna Carta: Why It Is Important to Sovereign Men and Women

Roger Davies

Published by TWON Publications, 2025.

THE MAGNA CARTA: WHY IT IS IMPORTANT TO SOVEREIGN MEN AND WOMEN

First edition. September 14, 2025.

ISBN: 979-8232691967

Written by Roger Davies.

Table of Contents

This book is dedicated to those who remember the spirit of Runnymede, who refuse false authority, and who teach their children that freedom is by birth, not by grant.

It is written to inspire thought, not to provide legal advice. Each reader is responsible for their own actions and decisions.

"When rulers break faith, Magna Carta reminds the people that obedience ends."

Introduction

Freedom is the natural birthright of every man and every woman. It is not given by government, it is not granted by parliament, and it is not bestowed by a king or queen. Freedom comes from the Creator and exists in the living soul. No statute, no decree, no office can take it away. Yet throughout history, men in power have sought to bind others in chains of law, contract, and fear.

In 1215, something extraordinary happened. A line was drawn between ruler and ruled. King John of England, one of the most tyrannical kings to ever sit upon a throne, was forced by his own barons and by the will of the people to place his seal upon a charter. This was the Magna Carta, the Great Charter of Liberties. It was not a gift. It was a recognition of a truth that had always been there: no man is above the law, not even the king.

Many have been taught that Magna Carta is a relic, a curiosity of medieval history. Schools mention it briefly, if at all, presenting it as a dusty scroll locked in a glass case. Politicians speak of it as a noble symbol, but nothing more. Judges and officials insist it has been repealed, replaced, or rendered obsolete. Yet this is deception. The principles of Magna Carta are eternal. They cannot be repealed because they do not come from parliament or from a crown, but from natural law itself.

The men of 1215 did not create freedom, they confirmed it. They did not invent trial by jury, lawful rebellion, or the right to property.

These rights existed already. Magna Carta was the written witness, a covenant between the people and authority. It stands as evidence that men and women are sovereign by birth.

Article 61, the security clause, declared that if the king broke the Charter, the people had the lawful right to rebel, to withdraw their consent, and to hold him to account. This is not mere history. It is a living principle: when rulers act in dishonour, the people are not bound to obey. Consent makes law, and when consent is withdrawn, authority falls.

For sovereign men and women today, Magna Carta is proof that we do not stand alone in our claims. We are heirs to a tradition of resistance, to a covenant sealed in blood and honour eight centuries ago. When we say that we do not consent to unlawful statutes, when we say we are living men and women, not corporate persons, we echo the spirit of Runnymede.

Magna Carta tells us that law is not whatever parliament declares. Law is rooted in truth, in natural justice, in the ancient customs of the people. Trial by jury was recognised as the shield of liberty. No fine or punishment could be imposed except by the judgement of one's peers. No man could be imprisoned without lawful cause. No tax could be levied without consent. These were not gifts from the king. They were acknowledgements that sovereignty rests with the people.

Yet look around today. Taxes are taken without consent. Courts operate as commercial forums where judges enforce contracts rather than justice. Men and women are imprisoned on the order of bureaucrats without true jury trial. Police enforce policy, not law.

Governments claim that the Magna Carta has no force, while at the same time quietly invoking its principles when it suits them. The deception is clear: they want the people to forget their birthright.

This book is written to awaken remembrance. It is for those who feel in their hearts that something is wrong, that life under constant regulation, taxation, and surveillance is not freedom. It is for those who know that the system depends on deception and consent. It is for sovereign men and women who wish to reclaim their standing.

We will examine Magna Carta not as a museum piece, but as a living covenant. We will see how Article 61 empowers lawful rebellion against tyranny. We will explore trial by jury as the true court of the people. We will compare common law with statute and show why one binds rulers while the other only binds those who consent. We will expose the illusion of repeal, showing how the state has tried to bury Magna Carta, yet never erased its authority. We will share stories of men and women who have invoked Magna Carta in modern times and unsettled officials with honour and truth.

Each chapter will reveal how Magna Carta supports the standing of the sovereign individual. We will uncover its maxims and principles and apply them to daily life. We will see how notices, conditional acceptance, and honourable questions are rooted in the same truths that compelled a king to kneel at Runnymede.

This is not about nostalgia or sentiment. It is about recognising that the battles of the past continue today. The names have changed, but the struggle is the same: freedom versus control, sovereignty versus subjection, natural law versus corporate statutes.

Magna Carta is not history, it is heritage. It is the inheritance of every man and woman who refuses to live as property.

The system will tell you that Magna Carta is dead. But ask yourself: can a parliament of men repeal truth? Can a statute erase your birthright? Can a corporation undo the covenant between people and authority? The answer is no. The lie of repeal is designed to break your spirit, to make you forget what is yours. Once you remember, the illusion collapses.

Magna Carta is a mirror. When you look into it, you see not a king, not a government, not a judge in robes, but yourself. A free, sovereign man or woman, born with unalienable rights. Those rights are older than parliaments, older than monarchs, older than the very paper upon which they are written. They come from the Creator, from life itself.

This book will remind you of that truth. It will encourage you to stand in honour, to speak calmly, and to question every claim of authority. It will show you how Magna Carta remains a living shield and a sword for those who choose freedom. It will not give you sovereignty, for you already have it. It will remind you of who you are.

The Great Charter still speaks. Will you listen?

Chapter 1: The Birth of Freedom

Every man and woman alive today carries within them the inheritance of a moment in time that altered the course of history. In the summer of 1215, on the meadows of Runnymede beside the River Thames, the foundations of modern freedom were confirmed. This was the sealing of the Magna Carta, the Great Charter, a covenant that still speaks across the centuries.

The story is often told in schools as if it were a minor squabble between King John and his rebellious barons. Teachers dismiss it as a quarrel over feudal rights, taxes, and privileges. The truth is far greater. What happened in 1215 was not merely a negotiation. It was a recognition that no ruler may stand above law, and that the people, through their customs and through natural justice, hold sovereignty.

To understand Magna Carta, one must first understand the world that gave birth to it. England under King John was a land burdened by heavy taxation, arbitrary punishment, and constant conflict. John had lost lands in France, drained the treasury, and demanded more from his subjects to fund his wars. He seized property at will. He fined men without cause. He imprisoned rivals and demanded ransoms. Even the church turned against him, placing the kingdom under interdict.

The barons, weary of tyranny, gathered their strength. Yet they were not alone. Behind them stood townsmen, knights, and common folk who had suffered under John's greed. Their demand was simple: the king must be bound by law. He must acknowledge that his power was not absolute.

This was a radical idea. Across Europe, monarchs claimed divine right. They declared themselves above law, answerable only to God. Subjects were treated as property of the crown. Yet at Runnymede, this illusion was broken. The king, sword in hand, was compelled to place his seal upon a document that said, in clear words, that even the monarch must obey the law of the land.

Clause by clause, the Charter set limits. It declared that no free man could be imprisoned or stripped of his rights without lawful judgement by his equals. It demanded that justice must not be sold, denied, or delayed. It confirmed that taxation required consent. It stated that the church must be free from interference. It restrained the abuse of feudal dues, inheritance, and marriage rights.

But most importantly, it introduced a principle that would echo through history: power is not above law. Authority must answer to justice. This truth, sealed into parchment in 1215, is the foundation upon which sovereign men and women stand today.

From a sovereign perspective, Magna Carta was never about the barons alone. It was about the living people of England. The Charter gave written recognition to rights that already existed. Men and women were born free. They carried duties of honour, not chains of servitude. Magna Carta was simply the written witness of that truth.

Yet the rulers of the world prefer people to forget. They tell us that Magna Carta was repealed, that it was a medieval relic, that it has no place in the twenty-first century. They hope you will accept that lie, for if you do, you surrender your inheritance. If you believe the Charter is dead, you will no longer use it as a shield.

But the Charter is not dead. It is alive in every man and woman who refuses to submit to unlawful power. It is alive in every demand for trial by jury. It is alive in every refusal to pay unlawful tax. It is alive in every man and woman who declares: I am sovereign, not subject.

Consider Article 61, the security clause. It placed in writing that if the king broke the Charter, the people had lawful cause to rebel, to withdraw their obedience until justice was restored. Think about this. The very heart of Magna Carta is not obedience to authority, but the right to withdraw consent when authority breaks the law. That is sovereignty. That is the living truth hidden in plain sight.

The modern system hates Article 61. Judges call it obsolete. Politicians pretend it never existed. Yet the words remain written. They cannot erase them. And even if they burned every copy, the principle endures. No man has duty to obey an unjust ruler. No woman is bound to comply with unlawful statutes. Magna Carta is the written evidence of this eternal truth.

The meadow of Runnymede was not the end of struggle. John sought to annul the Charter within months, calling upon the Pope to declare it void. War followed. Yet the idea could not be killed. Magna Carta was reissued by later kings, confirmed again and again, and invoked throughout the centuries whenever rulers overstepped their bounds.

For sovereign men and women today, this is the lesson: power fears the truth of Magna Carta, but it cannot escape it. The Charter is evidence of consent withdrawn, of sovereignty confirmed, of freedom remembered. It is not a relic. It is a reminder.

Magna Carta was not a perfect document. It spoke in the language of its time. It dealt with land rights, feudal duties, and the disputes of a medieval kingdom. Yet hidden within those lines is the seed of universal freedom. What began as a charter forced upon one king grew into a principle that limits all rulers.

The centuries that followed proved this. Again and again, when kings sought to overreach, men and women turned back to Magna Carta. When Charles I tried to govern without parliament, he was reminded of the Charter. When James II was driven from the throne, Magna Carta was invoked to justify resistance. Across the ocean, the American colonists looked to it when declaring independence. They wrote its spirit into their own Bill of Rights.

This endurance is proof that Magna Carta is more than parchment. It is living testimony that the people are sovereign. It is why governments today try to downplay it, teaching children to view it as a relic instead of a shield. If men and women realised that they already hold this power, the whole structure of control would begin to fall.

Look closely at the principles confirmed in 1215. No imprisonment without lawful judgement. No taxation without consent. Trial by jury. The right to lawful rebellion. These are not statutes that can be repealed at the whim of a parliament. They are maxims of natural law. They are truths recognised by every culture, in every age. They are as real today as they were eight centuries ago.

Consider what this means in practice. When a government claims it has the power to tax your labour without consent, Magna Carta says otherwise.

When a court seeks to punish you without a jury of your peers, Magna Carta says otherwise. When authority enforces statutes that cause harm or deny justice, Article 61 says you have the lawful right to withdraw obedience.

The modern state wants you to believe that freedom comes from licences, benefits, and rights granted by officials. But Magna Carta reminds us that freedom comes by birth. It is not given, it is recognised. The Charter was a moment when rulers were forced to admit this truth on record. That admission cannot be undone, no matter how often they claim repeal.

Stories through history reinforce this. Jurors have refused to convict men and women under unjust laws, citing their duty under Magna Carta. Rebels and reformers have invoked it in their petitions and protests. Even judges have quoted it, sometimes reluctantly, to affirm that justice cannot be sold or denied. Each time, Magna Carta has stood as a reminder that authority has limits.

Sovereign men and women today stand in the same tradition. When we challenge unlawful claims, when we refuse to act as corporate fictions, when we demand trial by jury, we walk the path laid down at Runnymede. We are not inventing something new. We are remembering what is ours.

This is why Magna Carta matters. It is not simply history. It is heritage. It is evidence. It is the living record that no man is subject unless he consents, that no woman is bound unless she agrees. It is the written covenant that rulers are beneath law, and that law itself is rooted in natural justice, not in statutes written for profit.

The meadow at Runnymede was more than a political gathering. It was a moment of revelation.

A king was made to bow before truth. That truth has never died. It lives in every act of honour, in every jury that defies an unjust judge, in every man and woman who refuses unlawful commands.

Magna Carta is not finished. Its story continues with us. Each generation must claim it anew. Each sovereign man and woman must remember that they are free by birth. The Charter is the written witness. We are the living proof.

Chapter 2: The King Bound by Law

The most powerful truth confirmed by Magna Carta is simple yet world-changing: the king himself is subject to law. In 1215 this was a thunderclap. Across Christendom, monarchs ruled by claiming divine right. They declared themselves answerable only to God. Their word was law, and the people were expected to kneel.

But at Runnymede, King John was forced to admit that even he could not stand above justice. By placing his seal on the Charter, he acknowledged limits. He agreed that his power was not absolute, that he could not fine, imprison, or tax without lawful cause and the consent of the realm. For the first time, it was written that the king was beneath law.

Why does this matter today? Because the modern system still tries to cloak itself in the old illusion. Governments, parliaments, and courts act as if they hold unlimited authority. They pass endless statutes. They tax without asking. They fine without proof. They behave like kings of old, cloaked in robes and titles, expecting obedience. Yet Magna Carta still whispers across the centuries: no one is above law, not even the crown.

For sovereign men and women, this is the cornerstone. Authority only exists with consent. Rulers who act without honour are usurpers, not masters. A government that taxes without agreement is no different from John when he extorted his subjects. A judge who fines without a jury is no different from John when he imprisoned rivals. Magna Carta proves that such acts are unlawful, then and now.

Clause after clause confirms the principle. "No free man shall be seized or imprisoned except by the lawful judgment of his equals or by the law of the land." That line alone destroys the illusion of arbitrary power. It means that neither king nor government can punish without the consent of the people. Not consent once given for all time, but consent in each case, judged by peers.

Another clause declares: "To no one will we sell, to no one deny or delay, right or justice." Think about this. Justice is not a service for sale. It is not to be withheld or postponed at the will of a ruler. Yet today, courts sell justice through fees, licences, and fines. They delay cases for years. They deny trials by jury. They have broken the very words they claim to revere.

The king bound by law means that all who claim to rule in his name are equally bound. Parliament sits under the crown, not above the people. Judges act under the royal seal, not outside of it. Every police officer swears an oath to serve under law, not to stand over the people. When any of them act beyond law, they act in dishonour, and their orders carry no authority.

This is the forgotten truth. Authority is not absolute. It is conditional. It depends on honour and on consent. The Charter shows us that even the highest office must obey. This is why sovereign men and women reject unlawful commands. They know that rulers who forget Magna Carta are not legitimate rulers at all.

The lesson of 1215 is this: once a king admitted he was bound, every future ruler is bound also. No parliament can erase this. No statute can undo it. It is not simply a historical event. It is a principle of natural law, written on parchment for all to see.

When King John sealed Magna Carta, he did so unwillingly. He was cornered, forced into submission by the barons and by the weight of truth. Within weeks he tried to break his word, appealing to the Pope to annul the Charter. But the act was done. Once admitted, the principle could never be erased.

This is the nature of truth: once spoken, it cannot be unsaid. Once a king has acknowledged that he is beneath law, no crown can ever again claim otherwise. Rulers may deny, they may pretend, they may threaten, but the record remains. Magna Carta stands as a witness that the highest authority is subject to justice.

Over the centuries, this principle was tested again and again. Monarchs who tried to ignore it faced rebellion. Charles I, lost his head when he refused to accept limits. James II was cast from the throne when he broke the covenant. Each time, Magna Carta was invoked. Each time, the people reminded rulers that their power was conditional.

For sovereign men and women today, this history is not distant. It is a guide. When officials demand obedience to statutes that cause harm or deny rights, remember that even kings were told no. When governments act as though their will is law, remember that Magna Carta binds them still.

Consider the words of Article 61, the security clause. It provided that if the king failed to honour the Charter, a council of the people could lawfully resist him until justice was restored. This is lawful rebellion, not treason. It shows that obedience is not absolute. It is conditional, tied to honour and justice. If rulers break the covenant, the people are not bound.

This is the essence of sovereignty: no man is subject by birth, no woman is bound without agreement. Authority is lent, not owned. Once misused, it is withdrawn. Magna Carta confirms this not as a theory, but as a fact of law.

Think of what this means in our daily lives. When a council demands tax without contract, you have the right to question. When a court fines without jury, you have the right to challenge. When a government passes statutes that strip freedoms, you have the right to withdraw consent. Each act of defiance is not rebellion against law, but obedience to higher law, the same law that bound King John.

The system fears this knowledge. That is why schools skim over Magna Carta in a few lines. That is why officials insist it has no force. They know that once men and women understand the Charter, they will stop obeying unjust demands. Knowledge is the key that opens the chains.

The king bound by law means something more than politics. It means equality before truth. No robe, no crown, no office makes a man greater than his neighbour. Authority exists only with consent. Titles are masks. Remove the mask, and every ruler is simply a man or a woman, subject to the same law of honour as everyone else.

This chapter closes with a question. If even a king in 1215 was bound by law, how much more are today's officials bound? If John was compelled to admit his limits, why should parliaments, corporations, or judges pretend otherwise? They are not above law. They never were. Magna Carta proves it.

Chapter 3: The People's Veto

Among the many clauses of Magna Carta, none is more feared by rulers than Article 61. Historians call it the "security clause." Sovereign men and women call it the people's veto. It is the single line of parchment that shatters the illusion of absolute authority and proves that obedience to rulers is conditional.

To understand its power, we must recall the moment it was written. The barons who confronted King John did not trust him. They knew his nature, slippery and deceitful. They knew that once he placed his seal on the Charter, he would try to wriggle free. To prevent this, they demanded a safeguard. Article 61 was that safeguard.

It stated that if the king or his officers broke the Charter, a council of twenty-five barons would have the right to declare lawful rebellion. They could seize castles, lands, and possessions until justice was restored. More than this, it declared that all men and women of the realm were free to support the council in their resistance without penalty.

Read those words carefully. They are nothing less than an admission that obedience is not permanent. Authority is conditional. When the covenant is broken, the people are free to withdraw consent. Not secretly, not shamefully, but lawfully. Article 61 turns rebellion into duty. It transforms defiance into honour.

Modern historians dismiss this clause. They say it was temporary, that it was repealed within months, that it has no standing. But ask yourself: can truth be repealed? Can the right of a man or woman to resist tyranny expire?

Can a parliament erase the principle that authority is bound by honour? Of course not. Article 61 is eternal because it expresses natural law.

For sovereign men and women today, Article 61 is a cornerstone. It is written proof that when governments break their trust, lawful rebellion is not only permitted but required. It is the evidence that consent can be withdrawn. It is the people's veto against tyranny.

Look around at our world. Taxes are levied without genuine consent. Courts punish without juries. Statutes are passed that strip freedoms, regulate natural rights, and criminalise peaceful men and women. These are breaches of the Charter, breaches of the covenant between rulers and people. Article 61 tells us that when breaches occur, the people are no longer bound.

This is why the system insists Article 61 is obsolete. They fear what would happen if people believed otherwise. They fear that men and women would stop complying with unlawful statutes, that they would withdraw consent, that the entire illusion of authority would collapse. So, they call it a relic. They tell you it is gone. But the words remain, carved into history.

Some have already acted upon this truth. Notices of lawful rebellion have been issued by men and women who refuse to stand as subjects of unlawful government. These notices declare allegiance to the Charter and withdrawal of consent from statutes that breach it. Officials ignore them in public but take them seriously in private. For when a man or woman stands in honour upon Article 61, they stand upon unshakable ground.

The principle is simple. Authority exists only while it keeps faith. Once it acts in dishonour, the bond is broken. The people are no longer bound. This is the heart of sovereignty. Article 61 is not a weapon of violence but of clarity. It says: when rulers betray trust, obedience ends.

When we speak of Article 61 today, we are not dealing with dry history. We are dealing with a living principle that exposes the fraud of modern authority. Officials say that rebellion is treason. They hope the word frightens you into silence. Yet Article 61 proves the opposite. When rulers break trust, it is loyalty to resist. Lawful rebellion is not treason. It is obedience to higher law.

Think of what this means. If a tax is demanded without consent, it is a breach of the Charter. If a man is imprisoned without jury trial, it is a breach of the Charter. If a statute strips natural rights from the people, it is a breach of the Charter. In every case, Article 61 declares that the people are free to resist, free to withdraw consent, free to stand as sovereign men and women.

This clause also destroys the myth that the crown holds permanent authority. Authority is conditional. It rests on honour. The moment it is abused, it collapses. Article 61 gave the people lawful tools to enforce this. Whether through councils, through notices, or through refusal to comply, the people may remind rulers of their limits.

Throughout history, echoes of Article 61 can be seen. When parliament defied Charles I, they invoked the spirit of the Charter. When jurors refused to convict men accused under unjust laws, they acted in its tradition.

When nations declared independence from empire, they stood on the same principle: the right of lawful rebellion against tyranny.

For sovereign men and women, the lesson is practical. Article 61 is not a call to arms, but a call to honour. Lawful rebellion begins with knowledge. It begins with refusing to consent to lies. It begins with asking questions: Where is the contract? Who is the injured party? What authority exists when the Charter has been broken? These questions expose the fraud. They strip power from officials who rely on silence and fear.

The system dreads this awakening. That is why Article 61 is mocked, hidden, or dismissed. But the more it is denied, the stronger it becomes. Every denial proves the fear of rulers. Every attempt to bury it reveals its enduring power. A truth that threatens tyranny cannot be erased.

Article 61 is the people's veto. It is the written reminder that no government, no parliament, no court has absolute authority. When honour is broken, obedience ends. Sovereign men and women today must hold this clause in their hearts. Not as history, but as living law. Not as a relic, but as a shield. Not as rebellion, but as fidelity to truth.

The meadow of Runnymede is far behind us, yet the covenant sealed there still speaks. The king was bound. Authority was limited. The people were free. That truth has not changed. It cannot change. It is natural law. Article 61 is its clearest voice.

Chapter 4: Trial by Jury – Shield Against Tyranny

One of the greatest gifts confirmed by Magna Carta is trial by jury. It stands as the people's shield, the line that no ruler should cross. The Charter declared that no free man shall be seized or imprisoned except by the lawful judgment of his equals or by the law of the land. Those words carry more power than armies. They place justice not in the hands of rulers, but in the hands of ordinary men and women.

In the world of King John, punishments were swift and brutal. A man could be fined, imprisoned, or killed on the whim of the monarch. No hearing, no defence, no protection. Magna Carta shattered that practice. It said that no man could be judged except by his peers, by equals who shared his standing. This principle confirmed that authority belongs to the people, not to the crown.

Trial by jury is more than procedure. It is sovereignty in action. When twelve men and women sit to judge a case, they are not mere servants of the state. They are the community itself, standing above rulers, judging even the law itself. A jury may refuse to convict if it believes a law is unjust. This is jury nullification, the hidden power that terrifies governments.

Officials never teach you this. They tell jurors they must follow the judge's instructions. They insist the law must be applied without question. Yet the truth is different. Magna Carta placed judgment in the hands of peers, not in the hands of judges. The jury decides not only the facts, but whether the law itself is fair. This power remains, whether officials admit it or not.

History proves it. Juries have refused to convict men accused under unjust laws. In England, William Penn was acquitted by a jury that defied a judge's orders, confirming the right of jurors to judge both fact and law. In America, juries refused to convict those accused under slavery laws, using their conscience to uphold justice over statute. Each act of defiance traces back to Magna Carta.

For sovereign men and women, this is vital. It shows that justice is not what rulers declare, but what peers decide. When you face a jury, you face equals who can judge not only your actions but the fairness of the law itself. No government wants you to remember this. They fear juries who think for themselves. They fear jurors who act as sovereigns.

The decline of jury trial in modern times is no accident. Governments push for summary justice, administrative hearings, tribunals, and plea bargains. They tell people it is quicker, cheaper, more efficient. In truth, it removes the shield. It denies the people their role. It replaces judgment by equals with judgment by officials.

When trial by jury fades, tyranny rises. Without juries, rulers are free to punish at will, just as King John once did. That is why Magna Carta placed trial by jury at its heart. It is the ultimate safeguard of freedom. It ensures that no man or woman is subject to authority without the consent of their community.

This chapter will show how juries embody sovereignty, how governments have undermined them, and how sovereign men and women may reclaim their power. It will reveal that trial by jury is not history, but a living right. A right that stands above statute, above parliament, above judges. It is the people's shield, the final word of justice.

The true power of the jury lies in independence. Twelve ordinary men and women, chosen from the community, hold the fate of an accused person in their hands. They are not bound by a judge's opinion. They are not bound by parliament's statutes. They are bound only by conscience, by natural justice, by what they know to be right. This is what makes the jury the people's shield.

Governments have always feared this independence. They have tried to weaken it in every age. Judges lecture jurors, warning them not to question the law. Officials threaten penalties for those who speak of jury nullification. Schools teach children that laws must always be obeyed. Yet history shows that when juries stand firm, tyranny falls.

Think of the case of William Penn in 1670. He was accused of unlawful assembly for preaching without permission. The judge demanded a guilty verdict. The jury refused. They declared Penn not guilty, even when threatened with imprisonment themselves. That verdict helped establish the independence of juries, a principle that spread to every corner of the common law world.

Think of the trials of men and women accused under oppressive laws. Juries have refused to convict those who defied unjust taxes, oppressive trade rules, or bans on free speech. By acquitting, they reminded rulers that the people, not officials, are the final judges. These acts of defiance kept alive the spirit of Magna Carta.

Yet today, juries are undermined. Many cases never reach them. Administrative hearings replace trials. Plea bargains pressure the accused into submission. Governments claim efficiency, but the truth is control.

Without juries, officials act as judge, prosecutor, and executioner all in one. This is not justice. It is tyranny reborn.

For sovereign men and women, the remedy is clear: demand trial by jury. Insist upon the right confirmed by Magna Carta. Refuse to be judged by officials alone. Stand firm until judgment is rendered by peers. This is not rebellion. It is obedience to higher law. It is the exercise of sovereignty in its purest form.

Trial by jury also protects against unlawful statutes. Jurors are free to refuse conviction when a law is unjust. They may decide that no crime has been committed if no harm has been caused. They may ignore statutes that conflict with conscience. This is why officials fear informed juries. They cannot control them.

The language of Magna Carta is simple: no free man shall be punished except by the lawful judgment of his equals. Not by a judge in robes. Not by a clerk in an office. Not by a bureaucrat applying regulations. By equals. By the community. By the sovereign people themselves.

This principle destroys the illusion of government supremacy. It places final authority not in palaces, parliaments, or courts, but in the hands of ordinary men and women. Every jury box is a throne of the people. Every verdict is a declaration of sovereignty.

The lesson is clear. If you wish to defend your freedom, defend trial by jury. Refuse to surrender it for convenience. Refuse to accept summary justice. Remember that without juries, rulers judge themselves, and tyranny is certain. With juries, the people judge rulers, and liberty lives.

Trial by jury is more than history. It is heritage. It is your shield against tyranny. It is the living proof that sovereignty rests with men and women, not with governments. Hold to it, defend it, and use it. For when the jury speaks, the people rule.

Chapter 5: Common Law vs Statute

Magna Carta confirmed a truth that existed long before parchment and seals: law is not created by rulers, it is recognised by them. This truth is the essence of common law. It is rooted in custom, conscience, and natural justice. It protects men and women by principle, not by decree. In contrast, statutes are written commands of governments, imposed from above, crafted by officials, and enforced for revenue. The two stand in opposition.

Common law is simple. Do no harm. Cause no loss. Commit no fraud. Honour your agreements. These maxims need no parliament. They arise from life itself. Every man and woman understands them. A child knows the difference between right and wrong, fairness and theft, truth and lies. Common law rests on this natural foundation. It belongs to the people.

Statute law is different. It multiplies endlessly, filling bookshelves with codes and regulations. One year's session of parliament produces more pages of law than the whole of medieval England. Most people cannot even read the rules that bind them, let alone consent to them. Statute law belongs not to the people but to governments, corporations, and officials.

Magna Carta recognised this divide. Its clauses affirmed that rulers were not free to impose their will as statutes. They had to respect the law of the land, which was the common law. When it declared that no man could be imprisoned without lawful judgment of his equals, it placed community judgment above royal command. When it said justice must not be sold or denied, it confirmed that law comes from truth, not profit.

Sovereign men and women understand this distinction. To live under common law is to live as a free being. To live under statute is to live as a subject of corporate control. Common law deals with flesh and blood. Statute deals with paper persons, legal fictions, and corporate entities. This is why every demand under statute is addressed to a name in capital letters. It is aimed at the Strawman, not the living man or woman.

Look at how statutes operate. A statute demands a licence to drive, though travel is a natural right. Another demands payment of council tax, though no contract exists. Another orders registration of property, as if the state owned your land. None of these statutes are rooted in harm, loss, or fraud. They are rooted in control and revenue. They exist to bind the Strawman, not the living.

Magna Carta strips away the illusion. It confirms that lawful judgment rests with peers, not officials. It confirms that consent is required for taxation. It confirms that justice is free, not sold for fees. These principles belong to common law. They expose the fraudulent nature of statutes that demand obedience without consent.

History shows the same conflict. Monarchs issued decrees, and people resisted by appeal to the common law. Parliaments passed statutes, and juries refused to convict. Time and again, the people have asserted that natural justice outranks official codes. Magna Carta stands as their evidence.

The difference is clear. Common law protects life, liberty, and property. Statute consumes them. Common law is eternal, for it arises from truth. Statute is temporary, for it arises from men. Common law belongs to all. Statute belongs to rulers.

This chapter will uncover how statutes have crept into every corner of life, how officials hide their lack of lawful authority behind paper, and how sovereign men and women may stand in common law, not statute. It will show that Magna Carta is not only history but proof that rulers are bound to common law, no matter what statutes they invent.

The system thrives on confusion. Officials speak of "the law" as if it were one single thing, but it is not. There is the law of the land, rooted in common law, and there are statutes, which are corporate policies written in legal language. By blurring the two, rulers trick men and women into believing they must obey every statute as if it were eternal law.

Consider taxation. Under common law, no man owes tribute unless he has agreed. Under statute, officials send demands to the Strawman, threatening penalties if payment is not made. The two are not the same. Common law requires consent. Statute presumes consent through silence. The difference is night and day.

Consider licences. A man does no harm by travelling freely. A woman commits no wrong by building a home on her land. Under common law, both acts are lawful. Statute transforms them into privileges. It demands payment for a licence and threatens punishment without one. Once again, the difference is clear: common law protects rights, statute sells them back.

The courts reveal this deception most clearly. When you enter a courtroom, the judge applies statutes to the Strawman. The language used—defendant, claimant, guilty, not guilty—belongs to statute. But if you stand as a living man or woman, demanding proof of contract and harm, you invoke common law. Judges fear this, for it exposes the fraud.

Magna Carta confirms the authority of common law. It did not create it; it recognised it. The Charter declared that justice cannot be sold or denied, that peers judge peers, that no tax is owed without agreement. These principles are eternal. They cannot be repealed by statute, because statutes are beneath them.

History proves this again and again. When juries refuse to convict under unjust laws, they are standing in common law. When men and women challenge statutes and demand contracts, they are standing in common law. When rulers admit limits to their power, they are bowing to common law.

This is why statutes are written in thousands of pages, while common law can be expressed in a few lines. Common law is simple: do no harm, cause no loss, commit no fraud, honour your agreements. Statute is complex, because it must disguise its true nature: control.

For sovereign men and women, the path is clear. Learn the difference. Refuse to act as the Strawman. Stand only in common law. When faced with demands, ask simple questions: Where is the contract? Who has suffered harm? What law of the land has been broken? If no answer is given, no duty exists.

This is not defiance of law. It is loyalty to true law. It is obedience to the principles confirmed at Runnymede. Magna Carta was the people's reminder that rulers are bound by common law, not free to invent statutes for profit. That truth has not changed.

The struggle between common law and statute is the struggle between freedom and control. One protects the living; the other binds the paper fiction. One requires consent; the other presumes it. One is eternal; the other is temporary. The choice lies with every man and woman.

The Charter shows the way. Stand in common law, and you stand free. Accept statutes blindly, and you live as property. The decision is yours. Sovereign men and women know where they stand.

Chapter 6: The Illusion of Repeal

Ask almost any official about Magna Carta and you will hear the same reply: "It has been repealed." Judges say it in court. Teachers repeat it in schools. Politicians claim it in debates. The message is clear—Magna Carta is dead, a museum piece with no force today. This is the illusion of repeal.

But let us pause and ask: how can truth be repealed? How can rights recognised as ancient and unalienable suddenly vanish because a parliament says so? Magna Carta was not the creation of parliament. It was not the invention of a crown. It was the written recognition of natural law, the law of the land that exists above rulers. No act of parliament can erase it, because no act of parliament created it.

The claim of repeal is a deception. It relies on the ignorance of the people. When officials say the Charter has been replaced, they speak of statutes and clauses, not principles. It is true that many specific feudal rules of 1215 have no use today. But the eternal principles—trial by jury, no taxation without consent, the right of lawful rebellion—cannot be annulled. They are not privileges granted by rulers but rights held by men and women by birth.

Consider the language used by governments. They say "the unrepealed clauses" of Magna Carta still stand, such as freedom of the church or the right to due process. They number them: four clauses left, the rest swept away. This makes the Charter sound like a hollow shell. Yet the truth is different.

Those surviving clauses point back to the whole spirit of the document. They confirm its continuing authority.

The deeper truth is this: even if every clause were repealed on paper, the principles would endure. Natural law cannot be erased by statutes. Do no harm, cause no loss, commit no fraud—these maxims cannot be annulled by majority vote. Nor can the recognition that rulers are beneath law. Once admitted, that truth stands forever.

Why then do officials insist upon repeal? Because they fear the Charter's power. They know that if men and women realised that Magna Carta still binds rulers, they would stop obeying unlawful statutes. They would withdraw consent. The system would collapse. Repeal is not a fact; it is a weapon of propaganda. It is meant to keep you silent.

This chapter will uncover the illusion of repeal, show how governments hide behind technical language, and prove that Magna Carta's authority is not diminished. It will demonstrate that repeal is an illusion built on statutes, while Magna Carta rests on natural law. It will arm sovereign men and women with knowledge: that no vote, no crown, no judge can take away what was written at Runnymede.

To understand the trick of repeal, we must look at how statutes are written. A parliament drafts a bill, declares that certain clauses are repealed, and stamps it with authority. On paper, the old words vanish. To the uninformed, this looks like power. But what has really changed? A statute may remove ink from books, but it cannot erase principles rooted in truth.

Take the example of taxation. Magna Carta declared that no tax may be levied without consent. Parliament has passed countless statutes demanding taxes without genuine agreement. They claim the Charter's words no longer apply. Yet when a man or woman asks, "Where did I agree to be taxed?" no statute can provide an answer. The principle stands untouched. Consent is required.

Or consider trial by jury. Magna Carta guaranteed that no free man shall be punished except by judgment of his peers. Modern statutes create summary courts, tribunals, and administrative penalties. Judges say the right to jury trial has been narrowed. Yet the principle remains. A living man or woman has the right to be judged by equals, not by officials. No statute can erase that truth.

The illusion of repeal is maintained by language. Officials use words like "obsolete," "archaic," and "replaced." They say Magna Carta belongs to history, while modern law is superior. This is sleight of hand. They shift your focus from principles to paperwork. They want you to forget that Magna Carta was never a gift from rulers but a recognition of unalienable rights.

Even judges have admitted this truth when pressed. Some rulings concede that Magna Carta embodies principles of constitutional importance, principles that no repeal can touch. These quiet acknowledgements prove the deception. While the public is told the Charter is dead, the system quietly admits that its principles endure.

Why then is the illusion so carefully maintained? Because memory is power.

If the people remember that they are sovereign, the spell of statutes breaks. If men and women realise that repeal cannot destroy truth, they will stop obeying lies. Authority survives only because people believe it is absolute. Once they see the limits, obedience fades.

For sovereign men and women, the path is clear. Do not be fooled by the illusion of repeal. When told that Magna Carta is gone, ask simple questions: Can truth be repealed? Can natural law be erased by parliament? Can rights given by the Creator be withdrawn by a statute? The answer is always no.

The Charter still speaks. It speaks through every demand for consent. It speaks through every call for trial by jury. It speaks through every act of lawful rebellion against tyranny. Its words cannot be silenced because they reflect what is eternal.

The illusion of repeal collapses the moment you see it. Once exposed, it loses power. You remember that the rights of free men and women do not come from books, but from life itself. Magna Carta is simply the record, the witness, the seal. What it recognised in 1215 remains as true today as it ever was.

The king was bound. Authority was limited. The people were sovereign. That truth cannot be repealed.

Chapter 7: Success Stories and Case Studies

Magna Carta is not merely a parchment sealed in 1215. It is a living principle that continues to be invoked by men and women who refuse to live as subjects. Across the years, ordinary people have stood upon its truths and found strength in its words. These stories are rarely told by officials or taught in schools, yet they are proof that the Great Charter still has force when claimed with honour.

One of the earliest examples comes from the seventeenth century. William Penn, later founder of Pennsylvania, was arrested in London for preaching without permission. The judge ordered the jury to convict him, but they refused. They stood firm, citing their duty under Magna Carta to judge freely. Even when threatened with imprisonment themselves, they held their ground. Penn was acquitted, and the case helped secure the independence of juries in English law. This was Magna Carta in action.

Move forward to the eighteenth century. The American colonists invoked Magna Carta repeatedly in their resistance to British rule. They declared that taxation without consent was unlawful, pointing directly to the Charter. When they broke from empire, they wrote its principles into their own constitutions. Trial by jury, due process, and the idea that rulers are bound by law all trace back to Runnymede. Magna Carta inspired a people to reclaim sovereignty.

But the story does not end with history. In modern times, men and women across the world have cited Magna Carta in defence of their rights.

Some have stood in court and asked whether they were being judged under common law or statute. Others have issued notices of lawful rebellion, declaring withdrawal of consent from governments that break the covenant.

Officials mock these acts, calling them misguided. Yet their very hostility proves the point. If Magna Carta were truly dead, why would rulers fear its invocation? Why would they spend such effort ridiculing those who speak its name? The answer is simple: the Charter still binds, and they know it.

One man challenged a council demand for tax by asking whether consent had been given, citing the Charter's protection against unlawful levies. The case was quietly withdrawn. Another refused summary judgment in a magistrates' court, insisting on trial by jury as guaranteed by Magna Carta. Faced with persistence, officials abandoned the claim. These stories are whispered in private circles, but they are real. They prove that when invoked with honour, Magna Carta unsettles the system.

The key is knowledge and calm. Men and women who stand in anger often fall into dishonour, giving officials an excuse to punish them. But those who stand peacefully, asking simple questions rooted in Magna Carta, often find doors closing quietly. The system thrives on silence and fear. It falters when confronted with truth.

This first part of the chapter has shown a handful of examples, from William Penn to modern men and women who have resisted unlawful claims. Each story carries the same lesson: Magna Carta is not obsolete. It is a living shield.

When rulers break trust, when officials overstep, the Charter provides ground to stand upon.

The system hides these victories, but those who seek them can find them. Newspapers will never report when a demand collapses because an honourable man asked for proof of contract. Schools will never teach of cases where councils backed down after Magna Carta was invoked. Yet in private conversations, in community meetings, and in the testimonies of those who stood firm, the truth emerges.

Consider the mother who refused to fill out endless school registration forms, asking instead under what authority her child was compelled to be listed as property of the state. When officials threatened, she calmly replied with words from the Charter: justice must not be delayed, denied, or sold. In the face of her resolve, the school relented. Her child was taught at home under private agreement. Magna Carta gave her courage to stand.

Or the farmer who faced fines for using his own land without the correct licences. He issued notices of conditional acceptance, asking whether the Charter's principle of no taxation without consent had been breached. The case vanished. Officials chose not to press the issue, for they had no answer to give.

Then there are the jurors who, even in modern courts, have refused to convict under oppressive statutes. Some cases of protest, trade, or free speech ended with acquittals because jurors followed conscience over instruction. Though the judges warned them to obey the letter of statute, they remembered the spirit of Magna Carta: judgement must rest with peers, not with officials.

These stories prove a pattern. The system is bold when unchallenged, but weak when faced with truth. It thrives on the presumption that people will obey without question. When a man or woman calmly invokes Magna Carta, asks for proof of contract, or insists on trial by jury, the illusion is broken. Many cases fade away quietly, for officials prefer retreat to exposure.

Of course, not every story ends in victory. Some men and women suffer penalties, ridicule, or imprisonment. Yet even these struggles carry value. They remind others that freedom is costly, that sovereignty demands courage. And often, even where officials appear to win, the seed of truth is planted. Others hear, others learn, and the knowledge spreads.

Magna Carta's power is not in grand victories but in steady resistance. Each time a man or woman stands upon it, they continue the line of Runnymede. Each notice sent, each case challenged, each refusal to consent keeps alive the Charter's spirit. The victories may be quiet, but together they form a chorus that rulers cannot silence.

The lesson of these stories is simple. Magna Carta works when used with honour. It is not a magic word or a script. It is a covenant that must be claimed with truth. Those who shout in anger or argue in dishonour weaken their case. Those who speak calmly, ask clear questions, and stand on the Charter's principles often find strength.

The Charter is not dead. It lives in the actions of ordinary men and women. It is alive each time a parent defends their child, each time a farmer defends his land, each time a juror defends conscience. Success is not measured by headlines but by freedom reclaimed, however small.

This chapter closes with a reminder. The meadow of Runnymede was not the end of a struggle but its beginning. The victories of today are the continuation of that same spirit. Every sovereign man and woman who invokes Magna Carta becomes part of its living history. The Charter is not a relic. It is a shield waiting to be raised.

Chapter 8: The Crown and the Corporation

When Magna Carta was sealed in 1215, the word "Crown" meant the living king himself. It was the person of John, bound by oath and charter, humbled beneath law. Over the centuries, however, the meaning of "Crown" shifted. It no longer referred only to the monarch but to an abstract entity, a corporation that could never die. This transformation is at the heart of modern deception.

The idea of the Crown as a corporation was clever. A king may die, but a corporation endures. By turning the Crown into a legal entity, rulers created a mask that could pass from one monarch to another without break. This corporate Crown is not a living man or woman. It is a legal fiction, a perpetual office with its own personality in law.

Why does this matter? Because it changes the relationship between ruler and people. When John placed his seal on Magna Carta, he was personally bound. He, as a living king, acknowledged limits. But when the Crown became a corporation, responsibility was blurred. No individual could be held accountable. Officials could hide behind the corporate mask, saying "the Crown" acted, not they themselves.

This shift turned sovereignty into an illusion. Men and women were taught to obey "the Crown" as if it were a living sovereign. In truth, they were obeying a legal fiction. The living king had been replaced by a perpetual corporation. And corporations operate not in honour but in commerce.

Magna Carta stands against this trick. It reminds us that the original covenant was between living people and a living ruler. It was not with a company, not with a fiction, not with an office that can never die. Sovereign men and women today can look back to 1215 and say: our agreement was with a man, not with a corporation. We owe no duty to a legal fiction.

The corporate Crown gave rise to endless extensions: Crown corporations, Crown courts, Crown estates. Each operates under the assumption that the people are subjects of a perpetual entity. Yet each one is rooted in the same fraud: the replacement of flesh and blood with paper and ink.

Look at how the system presents itself today. Court cases are brought in the name of "the Crown." Land is held in trust for "the Crown." Taxes are demanded for "the Crown." But where is this Crown? You cannot see it. You cannot speak to it. You cannot question it as a man or woman. It is a mask worn by officials to conceal their actions.

This chapter will reveal how the corporate Crown has been used to extend control, how it departs from the original covenant of Magna Carta, and how sovereign men and women may strip away the mask to see the truth. The Crown is a corporation, not a sovereign. The people remain sovereign, not subjects.

The corporate Crown has one great advantage over a living king: it cannot die. Monarchs pass away, yet the Crown endures. This gives the illusion of unbroken authority. It allows governments to claim that the Charter sealed in 1215 binds only John and his heirs, while the modern Crown is something new, separate, and untouchable. This is deception.

The corporate mask cannot erase the covenant. The people never consented to transfer their agreement from a man to a fiction.

By changing the Crown into a corporation, rulers freed themselves from personal responsibility. A judge can say he acts for the Crown. A minister can say he acts under the Crown. A police officer can claim he serves the Crown. Yet none of them are the Crown. They are men and women hiding behind a legal shield. The Charter was made to bind rulers personally. The corporate Crown twists that truth into an endless excuse.

This is why modern authority feels cold, faceless, and mechanical. You do not deal with a man or woman in honour. You deal with departments, agencies, and offices. You are told to obey "the Crown," but no such living being stands before you. This is commerce, not sovereignty. It is administration of contracts, not law of the land.

Magna Carta exposes the fraud. It shows that the original covenant was with a flesh-and-blood king, forced to kneel before law. That covenant cannot be transferred to a fiction without the people's consent. And the people never gave such consent. The system relies on assumption, not agreement.

Consider the courts. Every criminal case is brought in the name of "the Crown." But when you ask who the claimant is, there is no living man or woman who steps forward. The judge hides behind the corporate Crown. The prosecutor hides behind it. The police hide behind it. No one accepts personal accountability. Yet Magna Carta demands accountability. It demands lawful judgment by equals, not punishment by fictions.

Consider the estates. Vast lands are held as "Crown property." But who is the Crown? Not the living monarch in flesh and blood. The land is controlled by trusts, corporations, and departments. The people are told they are tenants of the Crown. In reality, they are tenants of a corporate system that exists only on paper. The land belongs by natural right to the people, not to an artificial entity.

Sovereign men and women must remember this: authority without accountability is no authority at all. The corporate Crown is a mask. Remove the mask, and you see ordinary men and women acting as officials. They are bound by law like everyone else. They cannot escape responsibility by invoking a fiction.

This is the power of standing in honour. When you face an official, ask: Are you acting as a man or woman, or are you hiding behind the Crown? Where is the contract binding me to this corporation? Who is the injured party? These questions pierce the illusion. Officials dislike them because they cannot answer honestly without admitting the truth: the Crown is not sovereign, the people are.

The Charter of 1215 was a covenant of living beings. The corporate Crown is an invention designed to shift power. It is a trick, nothing more. The sovereign man or woman owes it no duty.

The chapter closes with a reminder. The Crown is a mask. The corporation is a fiction. The living king was bound at Runnymede, and through him all rulers remain bound. The people never surrendered their sovereignty to paper. They remain free. Magna Carta is their evidence.

Chapter 9: Maxims of Magna Carta

Every great charter, covenant, or law rests on principles. These principles are not always written in the exact words of the text, but they shine through its meaning. Magna Carta is no different. Within its clauses lie maxims—short truths that express eternal law. For sovereign men and women, these maxims are more valuable than any statute book. They remind us who we are, what we owe, and what rulers may never take.

The first maxim is simple: No man is above the law. This was the heart of Runnymede. When John sealed the Charter, he admitted he could not rule by whim. He was subject to the same law as his people. This maxim destroys the illusion of divine right and modern supremacy of parliament alike. It confirms that every official, from king to constable, is bound by the law of the land.

The second maxim flows from the first: Law belongs to the people, not to rulers. Magna Carta made clear that lawful judgment rests with peers, not officials. The law of the land is not what parliaments declare, but what communities recognise through conscience and custom. This maxim places sovereignty with the people. It means that government has no authority unless the people consent.

The third maxim is one we have already seen in practice: No taxation without consent. John demanded scutage and other levies without agreement, and the barons rebelled. The Charter declared that no tax could be imposed without common counsel. This maxim stands today.

A demand for money without proof of contract is not law, but theft. Consent is the foundation of lawful tribute. Without it, rulers have no claim.

A fourth maxim follows: Justice must not be sold, denied, or delayed. This clause was written plainly in the Charter. It tells us that justice is a right, not a commodity. Yet modern courts sell justice daily through fees, licences, and fines. They deny justice through technicalities. They delay it for years while cases gather dust. Every such act is a breach of this maxim, a violation of Magna Carta.

Another maxim is at the heart of sovereignty: The people may lawfully rebel against tyranny. This is Article 61, the security clause. It tells us that obedience is conditional. When rulers act without honour, men and women may withdraw consent. This is not rebellion against law, but loyalty to higher law. It is a duty to truth and to the community.

These maxims are not mere words. They are living truths. They form the bedrock of sovereignty. Each maxim reflects natural law, the law that exists before and above statutes. A child understands them. A community thrives when it honours them. A ruler falls when he breaks them.

Part 1 of this chapter has laid out some of the central maxims: no man above law, law belongs to the people, no taxation without consent, justice must not be sold or delayed, and lawful rebellion against tyranny. These are the foundations of freedom. In Part 2 we will explore how sovereign men and women can apply these maxims in daily life, using them as shields against unlawful authority and as guides for honourable living.

The maxims of Magna Carta are not only for history books. They are guides for daily life. When a man or woman remembers them, they stand taller, speak calmer, and act with confidence. They know where the limits of authority lie, and they know that truth stands with them.

Take the maxim that no man is above the law. This applies not only to kings but to every official. When a police officer demands obedience without cause, this maxim reminds us that he is not master but servant. When a judge acts as though his word is final, this maxim reminds us that he too is bound. It strips away the illusion of supremacy and restores balance.

The maxim that law belongs to the people is equally powerful. It means that true law is not written in endless statutes but in the conscience of the community. A jury embodies this. Twelve men and women may decide that a statute is unjust and refuse to convict. They are applying the maxim directly, showing that the people hold the final word.

The principle of no taxation without consent is perhaps the most practical of all. Every demand for payment should be tested against it. When a council sends a bill, ask: where is the contract? When officials seize wages, ask: where is the consent? Without agreement, there is no lawful claim. This maxim reminds us that tribute is voluntary, not compulsory, unless harm or loss has been proven.

The maxim that justice must not be sold, denied, or delayed exposes the fraud of modern courts. When fees are demanded before a hearing, the maxim is broken. When years pass before judgment, the maxim is broken.

When officials refuse to hear evidence, the maxim is broken. To remember this truth is to see clearly that much of what is called justice today is commerce dressed as law.

Finally, the maxim of lawful rebellion shows the path when rulers act in dishonour. It reminds us that obedience is not permanent. Consent may be withdrawn. A man or woman who refuses to comply with unlawful statutes is not a rebel but one who stands in truth. Lawful rebellion is not violence. It is the refusal to lie, the refusal to consent to fraud, the refusal to bow when honour is broken.

These maxims also guide how we live with one another. If no man is above the law, then each of us must act with humility. If law belongs to the people, then each of us has a duty to act in honour with our peers. If no tax is owed without consent, then we must respect each other's property. If justice must not be sold or denied, then we must give each other fair hearing. If lawful rebellion is a right, then we must support one another when truth is defended.

Magna Carta's maxims are simple, but they are powerful. They strip away the complexity of statutes and bring us back to what matters. They remind us that freedom is not granted but recognised, that authority is not absolute but conditional, and that sovereignty rests with the people.

This chapter has shown that the maxims of Magna Carta are more than phrases on parchment. They are living truths. They protect us when invoked and guide us when remembered. The rulers of the world would prefer we forget them. But once remembered, they cannot be erased. They are carved into conscience, eternal as truth itself.

Chapter 10: Standing in Honour

Standing in honour does not mean loud defiance or angry protest. It means calm truth. The system thrives on fear and aggression. When a man shouts at officials, they label him a troublemaker. When a woman acts in rage, they call her unreasonable. But when you speak calmly, ask simple questions, and remain peaceful, they are unsettled. They expect fear or fury. They do not know how to face honour.

Magna Carta itself was born of this principle. The barons did not storm the castle with swords alone. They demanded a charter, a written agreement, proof of honour. They stood together, calmly but firmly, until the king sealed the document. That is standing in honour. It is strength without violence, firmness without malice, truth without compromise.

For the sovereign man or woman, standing in honour begins with language. Speak plainly. Do not accept titles that do not belong to you. If addressed as a person, a resident, or a taxpayer, ask who is being addressed. Do not lie, do not play games, but do not accept roles that are not yours. Say: I am a man. I am a woman. I live, breathe, and stand under the law of the land.

Standing in honour also means refusing false benefits. Many traps of the system are offered as privileges. Licences, subsidies, entitlements—all come with conditions. They seem like gifts, but they bind you into contract. The maxim of law says that no one is obliged to accept a benefit. Standing in honour means politely refusing what does not belong to you, and accepting only what is given in truth.

Consider the courtroom. Officials expect silence until you obey. They expect quick answers to charges. They expect you to accept the role of defendant. Standing in honour changes the script. You ask: Who is making the claim? Who has suffered harm? Where is the contract binding me? These questions are not defiance. They are honour. They refuse lies without anger. They expose the fraud without insult.

This approach works because the system is built on assumption. It assumes you will play the role offered. It assumes you will respond to the Strawman name. It assumes you will plead. When you refuse calmly, the system falters. Officials do not know how to proceed without consent. Silence or aggression feeds them. Honour starves them.

Honour also protects the man or woman who stands alone. Others may mock, threaten, or ridicule. But truth spoken without anger is hard to dismiss. A calm man asking for proof of contract is harder to punish than an angry man shouting at authority. A woman who patiently repeats that she is living flesh and blood is harder to ignore than one who lashes out. Honour turns weakness into strength.

Part 1 of this chapter has set the foundation: standing in honour is the practical expression of sovereignty. It is the way of speaking and acting that makes Magna Carta more than history. It is the way of life that transforms knowledge into power. In Part 2 we will explore how notices, conditional acceptance, and everyday practice embody this principle, and how men and women today can use honour to stand free.

To stand in honour is not theory but practice. It must be lived in daily encounters, in written notices, and in every response to claims made against you. The most powerful tool is the notice. A notice is a simple declaration of truth, placed on the record. When an official presumes your consent, a notice corrects the presumption. When silence would be taken as agreement, a notice replaces silence with clarity.

Conditional acceptance is the most effective form of notice. It is not refusal, which can be painted as dishonour. It is acceptance upon conditions that must be met. For example: I will comply upon proof of obligation, proof of contract, and proof of authority. These words are calm, reasonable, and honourable. Yet they expose the weakness of the system, for such proof cannot be provided. The claim collapses.

This method echoes Magna Carta itself. The barons did not refuse the king's authority outright. They accepted it on condition that he sealed the Charter and obeyed its terms. When he broke the terms, they withdrew consent. That is lawful rebellion, and it is the highest form of standing in honour.

Honour also means patience. The system thrives on haste. Officials want instant compliance. They issue deadlines and threats. When a man or woman takes time, asks questions, and waits for answers, the system slows. Its momentum falters. Delay is a weapon when it is used with honour.

Practical examples abound. A man faced with a council demand replies with a notice asking for proof of contract. The council cannot provide it, and the matter falls silent. A woman in court refuses to plead until the injured party is identified. The judge grows uneasy, for without consent the case lacks foundation. These are not victories of force, but of honour.

To live in honour also means to keep records. Every notice, every reply, every question should be kept. Honour is not only in words but in evidence. If taken before a court, a man who produces a clear trail of notices stands stronger than one who merely protests. The record shows that he acted in good faith, that he asked fair questions, that he sought truth. The system fears records because they strip away its power to twist the story.

Another part of honour is restraint. When threatened, many feel the urge to lash out. But anger is a trap. It gives officials excuse to escalate. Restraint keeps you safe. Calm speech confuses those who expect rage. A simple statement— "I do not consent without proof of contract"—is stronger than hours of shouting.

Finally, standing in honour means teaching others. Sovereignty is not selfish. It is a duty to community. When you act with honour, you show others that it is possible. Children who see their parents speak calmly to authority learn courage. Friends who watch a man refuse unlawful demands without fear are inspired. Honour spreads by example.

The lesson of this chapter is clear. Knowledge of Magna Carta gives strength, but honour gives form to that strength. It is the practice that turns rights into reality. Without honour, knowledge becomes noise. With honour, knowledge becomes power.

Standing in honour is the sovereign path. It is the way to live free without violence, to resist without rebellion, to obey truth rather than lies.

Magna Carta was sealed in honour. So too must every sovereign man and woman seal their own standing, day by day, notice by notice, word by word.

Chapter 11: Freedom for the Future

The Magna Carta is often spoken of as something from long ago, an event sealed in wax on a meadow in 1215 and locked away behind glass. Officials prefer you to think of it in this way, as if it were only a relic, to be admired in a museum but never used in daily life. Yet the truth is different. Magna Carta is not finished. It is alive, and it demands that each new generation decides whether to carry it forward or to let it fade into memory. Freedom is never permanent unless it is remembered.

The rulers of today understand this well. That is why they spend so much effort controlling history. Schoolchildren are taught a thin story: that the Charter was a quarrel between a king and his barons, that it led in some vague way to modern democracy, and that only a few clauses remain. They are not taught about Article 61, the people's veto. They are not told that trial by jury is a weapon against tyranny. They are not reminded that taxation without consent is unlawful. Instead, they are taught to believe that government is the source of rights, that law flows from parliament, and that obedience is virtue. This is not education but conditioning. Forgetting is the tool of control.

Yet forgetting can be reversed, and that task belongs to sovereign men and women. Magna Carta is a flame that must be passed down from parent to child, from neighbour to neighbour, from community to community. It is not enough to read about it once or speak of it in private. It must be taught, shared, and lived. The barons of 1215 did not stand for themselves alone. They stood for their heirs, for all those who would come after them. If we do not do the same, the chain is broken and sovereignty is lost.

The home is the first school of freedom. Children should learn the maxims of law before they ever read a statute book. Do no harm. Cause no loss. Commit no fraud. Honour your agreements. These are the true laws of the land, older than kings and parliaments. A child who grows up hearing these truths cannot be easily deceived when officials tell him that rights come from licences, fees, or permissions. He will already know that freedom is by birth, not by government. Parents who speak of Magna Carta around the table do more to preserve liberty than any parliament.

Communities are the second shield. When men and women gather to share knowledge of sovereignty, the illusion of isolation breaks. The system wants each person to feel alone, to believe that resistance is futile and that no one else sees the fraud. But when people meet, even in small numbers, courage grows. Stories of notices served, taxes questioned, and courts unsettled are shared, and others learn they are not powerless. The flame spreads, and rulers fear it.

History proves this pattern. Magna Carta itself was not sealed once and then forgotten. It was confirmed again and again because the people refused to let it die. In times of civil war, they raised it as a banner. In times of tyranny, they demanded its words be read aloud. Even kings who hated it were forced to confirm it, for the people remembered. That is the secret: memory keeps freedom alive. Forgetting kills it.

This part of the chapter has laid the foundation. Freedom for the future depends on remembering, teaching, and sharing. Each generation must be told that Magna Carta is not history but heritage. The Charter is a living covenant, not a relic. In Part 2 we will explore the practical steps that men and women can take today to carry these truths forward—through notices, through education, through communities of honour—and how the next generation can be prepared to stand as sovereign, not subject.

If freedom is to endure, it must be practised. It is not enough to admire Magna Carta from a distance. The Charter must live in the choices of men and women today. Every act of honour, every notice served, every refusal to consent, every lesson passed to a child is a thread that keeps the fabric of sovereignty intact. The system counts on people forgetting to practise. Remembering is only the first step; living the truth is what carries it forward.

Practical steps begin with awareness. When an official letter arrives, do not respond with silence or fear. Ask questions. Where is the contract? Who is the claimant? What obligation is being enforced? Place these questions in writing, calmly and firmly. This is the modern way of echoing Magna Carta. The Charter declared that justice must not be sold or delayed. A man who demands proof of claim honours that principle in his own life.

Education is the second step. Formal schooling will never tell children the truth about sovereignty, for schools serve the state. That is why parents, families, and communities must take the role of teachers. Reading the words of the Charter together, discussing its maxims, and connecting them to daily life keeps the truth alive.

When a child asks why he must obey, a parent can answer: you must not harm, you must not cause loss, but no man or woman has authority over you without consent. That lesson lasts longer than any textbook.

The third step is community. Men and women who know the truth must not hide it. They must meet, speak, and share. A lone voice is easily mocked. A chorus is harder to silence. Community does not require grand assemblies; even small groups strengthen courage. When neighbours stand together, they create a shield. The rulers of the world are powerful only when people are scattered. When people gather, fear changes sides.

Another way of preserving freedom is through record. Notices, affidavits, and declarations should be kept, copied, and shared. These documents are not only tools for today but lessons for tomorrow. Future generations will look back at them as proof that their parents and grandparents did not submit quietly. Just as the barons left their seal on parchment, so too can sovereign men and women leave records for their heirs.

Living the Charter also means rejecting false authority in daily life. When pressured to sign away rights for convenience, refuse. When told to pay for permissions that should be natural, decline. These small acts of refusal create ripples. Each man or woman who refuses to bow to fraud inspires others to do the same. The strength of Magna Carta lies not in a single act of rebellion but in the daily refusal to consent to dishonour.

Freedom for the future requires vision. Imagine a community where children grow up knowing they are sovereign, where parents teach that rights come from birth, not from government, where officials are questioned politely but firmly at every turn, and where neighbours stand together. Such a community cannot be enslaved, for it remembers. This is the true legacy of Runnymede: not a document on a shelf, but a people who will not forget.

This chapter closes with a duty. The men of 1215 stood for their heirs. They sealed a covenant not for themselves alone but for the generations yet to come. Today the same duty falls on us. If we do not pass on Magna Carta, the system will erase it from memory. But if we speak it, live it, and teach it, freedom will survive. The future will inherit not chains, but truth. That is the task of sovereign men and women.

Chapter 12: The Sovereign Path

Magna Carta was not written only for the thirteenth century. It was sealed to stand as a covenant between rulers and the people for all time. Though officials now call it obsolete, it remains a signpost for those who seek freedom. It shows that sovereignty is not an invention of modern movements but a truth recognised eight centuries ago. The path of the sovereign man or woman is not a new road but the continuation of an ancient one. The meadow of Runnymede was the beginning, and every generation since has been asked whether they will walk that path or abandon it.

The first step on the path is knowledge. No man or woman can stand free in ignorance. Fear is born of confusion. When a letter arrives demanding payment, ignorance causes panic. When an officer gives orders, ignorance causes submission. Knowledge changes this. A man who has read Magna Carta knows that taxation requires consent. A woman who understands the Charter knows that justice cannot be sold or denied. Knowledge does not erase challenges, but it dissolves fear. Once you know the limits of rulers, their threats lose power.

This knowledge is not hidden in libraries. It begins with simple maxims. Do no harm. Cause no loss. Commit no fraud. Keep your agreements. These are the true laws of the land. When compared to the endless complexity of statutes, they shine with clarity. They cannot be repealed because they are not created by rulers. They are recognised by conscience. Every child knows them instinctively. Knowledge of these maxims is the foundation of sovereignty, and Magna Carta is their written witness.

The second step is honour. Many men and women make the mistake of confusing sovereignty with licence. They believe that to be sovereign is to ignore all duties, to take without giving, to escape all responsibility. This is not sovereignty but selfishness. True sovereignty is bound to honour. To stand free is to stand accountable for one's own actions. If you cause harm, you must answer for it. If you cause loss, you must restore it. If you make an agreement, you must keep it. Honour is what separates sovereignty from lawlessness. Without honour, freedom becomes chaos, and chaos gives rulers their excuse to tighten chains.

Honour is also the shield against ridicule. Officials mock those who invoke Magna Carta, calling them cranks or extremists. Media portray sovereign men and women as dangerous. Yet ridicule loses force when met with calm honour. A man who speaks plainly, without malice, who asks for proof of contract, who stands on the Charter's words, is harder to dismiss. His honour protects him better than any argument. A woman who calmly insists that no one is above the law, citing Magna Carta, reveals the dishonour of those who mock her. Honour is not loud. It is steady, and its steadiness unsettles authority more than anger ever could.

The third step is practice. Knowledge and honour mean little if they are not applied. The sovereign path is walked in daily acts, not only in moments of crisis. It begins with how you respond to demands. When a notice arrives claiming a debt, reply with conditional acceptance: I will comply upon proof of contract, proof of claim, proof of authority. This is not rebellion but honour. It is the same principle the barons applied in 1215: we will obey the king if he obeys the Charter.

When he broke it, they withdrew consent. Practice means living this truth daily, accepting only what is proven, refusing what is fraudulent.

Practice also means preparing. Keep records of notices, copies of correspondence, and declarations of truth. A man or woman who records their standing creates a shield for themselves and an inheritance for their children. Just as the barons sealed their demands into parchment, so can we place our truth into writing. Practice transforms belief into evidence.

The fourth step is clarity. The path of sovereignty is not easy. The system surrounds us with illusions and statutes that claim supremacy, courts that pretend to serve justice, officials who hide behind the mask of the Crown. To stay on the path, one must see through illusions. When a statute claims to repeal Magna Carta, ask: can truth be repealed? When a judge insists his word is final, ask: is he above law? When officials threaten penalties, ask: where is the injured party? Clarity comes from refusing to accept illusions at face value. The Charter itself was written to expose illusion—the illusion that a king was above law. Once exposed, the lie collapsed.

The sovereign path begins with these four steps: knowledge, honour, practice, and clarity. Each step strengthens the man or woman who takes it. Each step strips away fear. Each step echoes the courage of those at Runnymede. Magna Carta remains a signpost not because of ink on parchment but because it points to eternal truths. In Part 2 we will walk further along this path, seeing how sovereignty is lived daily, how challenges are met without fear, and how men and women can walk together so that freedom is never lost again.

The sovereign path is not a straight road without obstacles. It is full of challenges, traps, and attempts to draw men and women back into silence and submission. Yet each challenge is also a test. Every notice, every encounter with officials, every demand for compliance is an opportunity to stand in truth. The barons faced swords and threats at Runnymede. Today we face paper, threats of fines, and corporate language. The test is the same: will we bow, or will we stand?

Daily life offers countless chances to walk the path. When an official sends a letter addressed to the Strawman in capital letters, you can choose silence or compliance. Or you can choose the sovereign path. You can reply with honour, asking whether the letter is meant for the living man or for a fiction. You can demand proof of obligation. You can stand as one who knows the difference between legal person and living being. Each reply is a step forward.

The same is true in courts. The courtroom is designed to intimidate—robes, symbols, titles, and rituals all create the illusion of power. But when a man or woman enters calmly and asks, who makes the claim? Who has suffered harm? Where is the contract? —the illusion falters. The judge expects obedience. When faced with honourable questions, he is unsettled. He cannot answer without revealing the fraud. A single man in honour can shake a court built on presumption.

The sovereign path also requires patience. Many victories are not seen in public. They come quietly, when cases are dropped, when demands are withdrawn, when officials retreat rather than expose themselves. The newspapers do not report these moments, but they matter.

They are proof that honour unsettles authority more than defiance. A man or woman on the path must be ready to accept that many of their victories will be silent, known only to those who walk with them.

Walking the path is easier when it is not walked alone. Sovereignty may be individual, but community strengthens it. When families teach children the principles of Magna Carta, when neighbours share experiences, when groups gather to discuss notices and rights, courage grows. Each person realises they are not isolated. The system thrives on loneliness. The sovereign path thrives on unity.

There is also a spiritual side to the path. Sovereignty is not only political but moral. It reminds us that we answer first to conscience and to the Creator, not to parliaments or corporations. To walk as sovereign is to live in harmony with natural law. It is to treat others with fairness, to respect their rights as we demand they respect ours. Sovereignty without morality becomes arrogance. Sovereignty rooted in natural law becomes freedom.

The final duty of the sovereign path is to carry it forward. Just as the barons sealed Magna Carta for their heirs, so must we leave proof for ours. Notices, records, teachings, and examples are all part of this inheritance. A child who sees a parent refuse unlawful demands learns a lesson more powerful than any lecture. A community that preserves its own records of truth leaves behind evidence that sovereignty was never surrendered.

The sovereign path does not end in one lifetime. It is a road walked by generations. Each man or woman adds their steps to the trail. Each act of honour keeps the covenant alive. Each refusal to bow to lies strengthens the Charter's legacy. Magna Carta began the journey. It is for us to continue it.

This chapter closes with a call. Do not let the Charter remain locked in books or museums. Live it. Walk it. Teach it. Remember that the king was bound, that rulers are limited, that sovereignty rests with the people. The sovereign path is not easy, but it is the only road to freedom. To walk it is to honour those who stood at Runnymede and to prepare the way for those yet to come.

Final Notes

The story of Magna Carta is not finished. It began at Runnymede in 1215, when a king was forced to admit he was bound by law. It continued through centuries of struggle, rebellion, and renewal. It carried across oceans, inspiring nations to declare independence. It survived attempts to bury it, mock it, and repeal it. And now it rests in your hands.

What you choose to do with it matters. You can treat it as history, as the system wants, or you can treat it as heritage, as those who sealed it intended. The choice is yours.

The Charter is not about barons and kings. It is about men and women, flesh and blood, living souls who refuse to bow to lies. It is about sovereignty that exists by birth, not by grant. It is about natural law that cannot be repealed, no matter how many statutes are written.

You have read how trial by jury is a shield, how Article 61 is the people's veto, how no tax is lawful without consent, how no man is above the law, how justice cannot be sold or denied, and how standing in honour is the way to live free. These are not lessons for the past. They are duties for today.

The system will not remind you of this. It will try to make you forget. It will mock, it will threaten, it will drown you in paperwork and demands. Yet the truth is simple. Authority is conditional. Consent can be withdrawn. Sovereignty rests with the people.

The men of 1215 stood in honour for their heirs. They sealed a covenant not for themselves alone but for you. The question is whether you will do the same for those who come after. Will your children inherit silence, or will they inherit freedom?

The path is before you. Walk it with knowledge. Walk it with honour. Walk it with patience. Walk it with courage. Magna Carta still speaks. The king was bound. Authority was limited. The people are sovereign. That truth remains, waiting only for you to claim it.

Don't miss out!

Visit the website below and you can sign up to receive emails whenever Roger Davies publishes a new book. There's no charge and no obligation.

https://books2read.com/r/B-A-HHGNE-HYCXG

BOOKS 2 READ

Connecting independent readers to independent writers.

Did you love *The Magna Carta: Why It Is Important to Sovereign Men and Women*? Then you should read *Freedom by Rebuttal: How to Say No and Stand Free*[1] by Roger Davies!

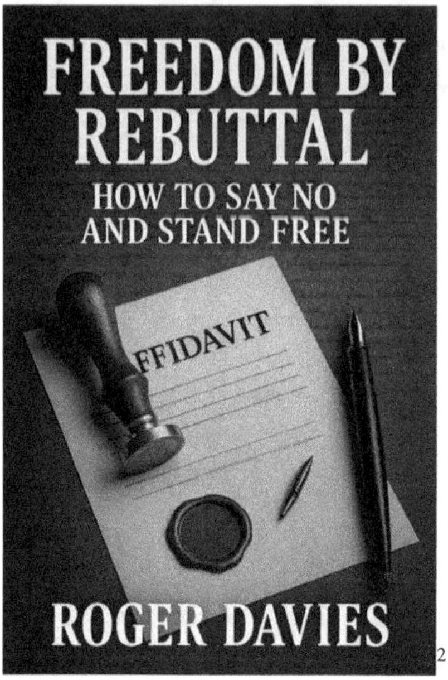

[2]

Freedom is not a gift from Parliament, courts, or officials. It is your birthright. Yet nearly every man and woman lives under taxes, debts, licences, and endless demands. The system does not force you with chains. It binds you with silence.

Freedom by Rebuttal shows how silence is turned into consent — and how you can take that consent back. This book is a practical guide to saying no lawfully, standing in honour, and using words instead of anger to collapse false claims.

Roger Davies takes you through the principles and practices of rebuttal step by step:

1. https://books2read.com/u/bxpM1v

2. https://books2read.com/u/bxpM1v

• How silence is treated as agreement in law• The Strawman trap and how to separate from it• Why honour is essential and how to keep it• The power of conditional acceptance: "Yes, on proof of claim"• Writing notices that shift the burden of proof back to the claimant• Turning notices into affidavits that stand as truth when unrebutted• Using rebuttal against council tax, banking debts, and fines• Responding to police and court summons with calm questions• Building community strength and supporting others who rebut

This is not a book of magic words or quick fixes. It does not promise that you will never face pressure. It shows you how to remain calm, how to act in honour, and how to put the other party on the record. When you rebut a claim with lawful notice, you remove presumption. When you conditionally accept on proof, you force the claimant to prove authority — and they usually cannot.

Freedom by Rebuttal explains that courts, councils, and banks rely on dishonour and silence to gain power. They thrive when you argue in anger or remain quiet in fear. Honourable rebuttal defeats both traps. It leaves you standing as a living man or woman, not a corporate fiction.

You will learn how to draft notices and affidavits, how to keep proper records, and how to respond when officials ignore your requests. You will see real examples of men and women who used rebuttal to collapse council tax cases, challenge false debts, and end claims in court.

This book is written for those who sense that something is wrong but are not sure what to do next. It offers practical tools that can be used daily — when a letter arrives, when a demand is made, or when you are called into court.

Freedom by Rebuttal is not rebellion. It is remedy. It is about placing your truth on the record, giving lawful notice, and refusing to be bound without contract. It is about taking back consent peacefully, with calm strength and patience.

If you are ready to stop living in silent agreement, if you are ready to face the system without fear, this book will show you how. The first step is simple: say no, and stand free.

Also by Roger Davies

Sovereign Foundations: Liberty, Rights, Consent

The Constitution of One: How the Bill of Rights Protects the Sovereign Man & Woman

From Subjects to Sovereigns: Reclaiming the Spirit of 1776

Liberty by Consent: Reclaiming Freedom Through the Law of Consent

Standalone

The Commonwealth Corporation: How Australia Was Turned Into a Business

The Legal Fiction: The Greatest Trick Ever Played on Humanity

The Sovereign Path: Living Free Beyond the System

Common Law: The True Law of the Living

Freedom by Rebuttal: How to Say No and Stand Free

The Magna Carta: Why It Is Important to Sovereign Men and Women

The Trust Game: Hidden Estates and the Cestui Que Vie Act

Freedom by Notice: Winning with Paperwork

The Hidden Contracts: How Governments Enslave the People

The Law of the Living: Admiralty Shadows and the Path to Sovereignty

About the Author

Roger Davies researches the crossroads of commerce, policy, and personal sovereignty. He writes for readers who sense there is more to the story, who are ready to replace fear with honour and paperwork with plain truth. When not writing, he helps men and women organise their records, challenge unfounded claims, and build communities grounded in mutual aid and responsibility.

www.ingramcontent.com/pod-product-compliance
Lightning Source LLC
LaVergne TN
LVHW022028200926
848481LV00007B/2595